I WAS A Stranger

I WAS A Stranger

A GUIDE TO BIBLICAL HOSPITALITY

What you have done to them,
you have done to me.

~ Jesus

MARILYN T. PARKER

I WAS A STRANGER: A GUIDE TO BIBLICAL HOSPITALITY

ISBN: 979-8-9857-509-3-5

Cover design by Roseanna M. White
Image from Shutterstock

PW Press
www.perseveringwomen.com
Email: marilynandbecca@perseveringwomen.com

Also by Marilyn T. Parker

The Struggle for Love: The Story of Leah
Available on Amazon

Watch for her new novel coming soon!

Marilyn T. Parker's author page
https://perseveringwomen.com/books/

I was a Stranger: A Guide to Biblical Hospitality
is dedicated to Lupe Urrea and Randy Clonts,
two shining examples of Christian hospitality.
Both went to heaven while I was writing this book.
I'm certain they were each greeted with, "I was a
stranger and you took me in.
Well done, my good and faithful servant."

I love and miss you both!

What Is This Book About?

Do you remember when Joseph and Mary went to Bethlehem? Joseph was desperately searching for a place for his young wife to give birth, but there was no room at the inn. I often think about that innkeeper. I'd wager he wishes he'd slept in the hay and given Mary his own bed. Imagine knowing for all eternity that you sent Jesus out to sleep with the cows and sheep!

I hope you and I are different than that man. We'll be looking at Matthew 25 in a minute, where Jesus said that whatever we've done to one of the *least* of His brothers or sisters, we've done to Him. Hopefully, we won't have to stand before Him in the judgment and explain why we let Him go hungry, or cold, or friendless.

I was a Stranger is a book about hospitality. No, it's not about how to throw the perfect holiday party or the proper way to set a table. This is a book about entertaining more than just friends and family. It's about Christian hospitality, opening our hearts and homes to people who are outside our circles. People who are different. It's about the heart of our country and the heart of our churches. It's about welcoming the strangers among us and why it's so very important to God that we do.

So, am I an expert on this subject? Well, if washing more sheets than the Marriot counts, then, yes. I am an expert. I was married to a pastor for forty years, and our house was always full. Sometimes with visiting preachers, sometimes with friends (or acquaintances who were soon to become friends), and sometimes with total strangers my late husband brought home off the street. I blame Bill for my long-standing battle with those stubborn extra pounds. I never knew who was going to walk through the door with him, so I had to cook accordingly. And everyone knows the people in Africa are going to starve if I throw anything away! For crowd-pleasing recipes, check out Cooking for Company at the end of this book.

I'll be honest, sometimes having a houseful of people was difficult. But it was always rewarding, and usually just plain fun. And it was a life-changing experience for my children. My kids grew up giving up their beds about ninety days out of the year. I did the math once! When we had long-term guests, it was more.

Now, some might think that's absolutely terrible. Making children give up their beds? Kids need their space! Right? True. But isn't it important that they learn to share that space? If we want our children to be generous adults, we must start by training them to be generous boys and girls.

Another benefit was my children learned to interact with people. Many visitors commented on how refreshing it was to see kids who were not only polite but able to carry on a comfortable conversation with grownups. This has served them well in their lives. They're very sociable adults who are able to engage with people of all walks of life.

I invited my children to share on my blog about how giving up their beds affected them as kids and into adulthood. Here's a segment of a humorous overview given by my oldest son, Peter.

> When we were kids we knew company meant seniority and a game of musical chairs was about to kick in.
>
> My parents' bed went to the adults visiting us. My mom and dad slept in Becca's bed. Becca slept in Sara's bed, and I ended up on a pallet on the floor. Sometimes the plan varied, but that was the gist of it—until Joshua came along, at which point he ended up on the floor as well.
>
> It was a given that we would give up our rooms for company, yet I don't ever recall hearing anyone complain. It was as normal as going to church four to five times a week.

Thank you, Peter. The part about going to church four to five times a week is a slight exaggeration (very slight).

Some of you may be hugging your Sleep Number controls right now, snarling, "No way am I ever giving up my bed." I'm not saying you have to. Maybe the occasion will never present itself, but are you willing if it does?

I have so many funny stories about my own experiences, I have to slip one in here and there. This is one of my favorites. I call this short story "Behind Door Number One."

> Years ago we were living in a small two-bed-

room, one-bathroom house. We lived in Arizona and the nights were comfortable, so our children slept on the screened-in porch when we had company. I wouldn't do that now—I'd pile them on the living room floor. But that was a different age.

We had two couples staying with us. One was an elderly couple, the Hiltons. Mr. Hilton was caring for his wife, who suffered from dementia—probably Alzheimer's. It didn't have a name at that time. She was bedridden. The other guests were newlyweds looking for jobs and a place to settle. My husband and I slept on the hide-a-bed in the living room.

Did I mention the house had one bathroom?

Well, that bathroom was situated between the two bedrooms. There was no outside entrance. You had to go through one of the bedrooms when nature called.

Another interesting thing about this situation—for different reasons both couples slept naked.

The old couple did so because the wife was incontinent and often wet the pad beneath her and her husband in the process. Mr. Hilton found it easier to sleep naked than change her nightgown and his pajamas during the night.

And the newlyweds? Well, don't ask me how I know they slept naked. After a couple of revealing late-night treks to the bathroom, my husband and I vowed not to drink anything after five PM.

The message of this book is this: whatever we do to others, we do to Jesus. When we entertain the *least* of Jesus's brethren, we entertain Him. Even naked people!

Sheep in Goats' Clothing

Matthew 25 brings this message home. So let's take a look at it. Because it's a lengthy passage, I'll summarize some of it.

Verse 31 talks about the Son of Man returning and gathering all nations to be *judged* (not anyone's favorite subject). He sets up two lines: one on the *right* for the sheep, and one on the *left* for the goats.

The King tells the guys on the *right* to come and inherit the kingdom that's been prepared for them from the foundation of the world.

He proceeds to tell them that He was hungry, and they gave Him food. He was thirsty, and they gave Him drink—and here's the one that we're interested in today—*He was a stranger, and they took Him in.* And the list goes on: naked, sick, in prison . . . the sheep stepped up—you get the picture.

Well, by now, these guys are shaking their heads because they know who Jesus is, and they know they haven't done any of these things for Him.

Oh, boy.

He must've gotten them mixed up with someone else! How embarrassing. Do they tell Him and get moved over to the "left-hand" lane? Things don't seem to be going so well on that side. Well, their conscience gets the best of them, and they tell Jesus there's been a case of mistaken identity.

Matt. 25:38 (NIV) records them asking, *"When did we see you a stranger and invite you in?"*

Here's the kicker. Jesus tells them something shocking (verse 40):

"Truly I tell you, whatever you did for one of the least of these brothers and sisters of mine, you did for me."

In the same passage of Scripture, Jesus turns to address the "goats." He says, *"I was hungry and you didn't feed me, thirsty and you didn't* give me *a drink. I was a stranger and you didn't* take me in.

The lefties plead their case.

"Lord, when did we see you hungry or thirsty or a stranger or naked or sick or in prison and did not minister to you?"

His answer: *"Whatever you did not do for one of the least of these, you did not* **do for me.** *Then they will go away to eternal punishment, but the righteous to eternal life" (verses 44–46).*

This scripture can be intimidating. It almost sounds as if we're saved by our good works. But we know we are made *righteous* by the blood of Christ. We're not sheep because we learn to bleat or because we wear a wool coat. We are *born again* that way. But sometimes God's sheep traipse around in goats' clothing. God takes our treatment of strangers very seriously.

Mi Casa Es Su Casa?

How big is your house? Do your children each have their own bedroom? What about a family room? A den? An office? Two offices? A laundry room? Two bathrooms? Three? More?

Wonderful! I'm happy for you. I truly am. But with abundance comes responsibility.

I want to tell you about some people who have very little but share it willingly and with open hearts.

Before my late husband passed away, our family ministered a great deal in Mexico. Bill's birthday was Christmas Eve, and going to Mexico was how we celebrated. Our children loved it. We would drive around with a van or a bus jammed full of food and clothing, giving to people who lived in shanties made of pallets or sticks—and sometimes cardboard! Not your dream house? Mine either.

If people had a one-room (room—not bedroom) adobe house, they were considered fortunate indeed. Most of us have closets bigger than that!

Their families were large (no local Planned Parenthood), and there were usually three or four generations in one small house. It reminded me of when I was a kid, and it was all the craze to see how many people you could cram into a telephone booth.

What's a telephone booth? It's a kind of glass box that

people used to step into to make a call when they were away from home. *Yes. Really.*

The average American house has doubled in size since the 1950s. What a blessing to have all that extra room! Most of the people of the world live in houses a fraction the size of American homes.

But however small their houses, I don't remember going to a home in Mexico where they didn't invite us in and offer us food. And these were not empty invitations like we so often give: "We've got to get together sometime. I'll call you."

They had very little, but they *insisted* on sharing what they had with us. There's nothing better in this world than beans and homemade tortillas in Mexico.

Sometimes we would have large groups of people with us: church youth groups or folks from the States wanting to help their southern neighbors. The Mexican women would set us at their tables and serve us like we were royalty. Actually, we were. We were sons and daughters of the King, and they treated us like they would have treated Him. They didn't do this out of their abundance. They did it out of their poverty, and yet it was obvious that they did it with great joy, counting it a privilege.

But it wasn't just visiting Americans they fed. They fed the poor in their neighborhoods also. Their houses were always full of people who had even less than they did. If they had any food at all, they were willing to share it.

There's a saying in Mexico: *Mi casa es su casa***.** My house is your house.

In America, I fear the saying might be "My house is *my* house." We consider our homes our private sanctuaries:

the place where we can close the doors and escape from the world—in front of our high-definition TVs.

But God sees it all, and He has something to say about it.

Practice hospitality to one another (those of the household of faith). Be hospitable, be a lover of strangers, with brotherly affection for the unknown guests, the foreigners, the poor, and all others who come your way who are of Christ's body. And in each instance do it ungrudgingly (cordially and graciously, without complaining but as representing Him). (1 Peter 4:9 Amplified Bible, emphasis mine)

How often do we see this in today's world? Not often, I fear. Oh, we'll have relatives over, although we often do even that grudgingly. We'll have the occasional dinner party, which usually ends up giving us heartburn, since the house has to be perfect, the food exotic, the guest list carefully planned—no inviting Aunt Bessie and Cousin June to the same party.

But how often do we open our homes to people who really need a place to stay for the night? Or ask people who are unable to reciprocate to share a meal?

Then Jesus said to his host, "When you give a luncheon or dinner, do not invite your friends, your brothers or sisters, your relatives, or your rich neighbors; if you do, they may invite you back and so you will be repaid.

*"But when you give a banquet, invite the poor, the crippled, the lame, the blind, and you will be blessed. Although they cannot repay you, you will be repaid at the resurrection of the righteous." (*Luke 14:12-14 NIV)

You will be repaid. God's good for it, and He will reward us at the resurrection. I'll take that over a huge empty house any day.

Another funny story! I call this one "Bring Your Own Padlock."

Years ago, my late husband and I were pastoring a small church in Silver City, New Mexico. We lived in a two-bedroom, one-bath house (a different one than in the last story. No going through the bedrooms to get to the bathroom!). Our three children all slept in one room. I think kids not having their own room might be considered child abuse now, but they survived quite unscathed.

A visiting preacher and his wife were staying with us. We gave the guests our king-size bed, and we slept in the living room on the pull-out. Practically sleepwalking, I got up in the night to go to the bathroom. When I left the bathroom, instead of going back to the hide-a-bed, I went to our bedroom and started to crawl into bed with the couple. I probably would have cuddled up to someone and slept there all night if I hadn't heard them giggling.

Needless to say, I was suddenly wide awake. Without a word, I slipped out and went back to the living room.

Breakfast was awkward!

The man and his wife became great friends in spite of my intrusion. The preacher told everyone that if they spent the night with the Thompsons, they should bring their own padlock. I never lived that one down.

Doing God's Will When It Seems Irresponsible

There's a story in the Bible about a preacher and a widow and her son that would make the headlines of every newspaper in America if it happened today: *Preacher Demands Last Bite of Bread from Starving Woman and Child.* It would be the lead story on every cable network.

Let me give you a little background before I jump in.

This story takes place during the reign of Ahab, King of Israel. Ahab was a really bad dude, and he had a wife who was even worse than he. Her name was Jezebel. Heard of her?

Israel had had a string of evil kings who had led God's people into idol worship and all sorts of reprehensible behavior.

And just when it seemed things couldn't get worse!

"Ahab son of Omri did more evil in the eyes of the LORD than any of those before him" (1 Kings 16:30 NIV).

See what I mean?

There was a prophet in Israel at that time named Elijah, and he didn't like what this bad king was doing to God's people. So he challenged him. But King Ahab wouldn't be worried about what some wild-eyed preacher from Tishbe had to say, so Elijah had to back up his words with some action.

Now Elijah the Tishbite, from Tishbe in Gilead, said to

Ahab, "As the LORD, the God of Israel, lives, whom I serve, there will be neither dew nor rain in the next few years except at my word. (1 Kings 17:1 NIV)

No rain? No dew? For how long? Years?

Well, that would get Ahab's attention, wouldn't it? You can read the entire account in 1 Kings chapters 17 and 18, but I'm focusing on Elijah's interaction with a particular widow.

Elijah was affected by this prolonged drought just like everyone else. On top of that, he had to hide from Ahab, who was trying to knock him off, thinking if the prophet was dead it might somehow start raining again.

As the drought spread, God had told Elijah to hide out next to a brook in the Kerith Ravine, east of Jordan, and He sent ravens with meat and bread in their beaks every morning and every evening to feed him. Not exactly Pizza Hut delivery, but Elijah didn't starve.

But eventually the stream dried up. No water. Now what?

God spoke to Elijah again:

"Go at once to Zarephath in the region of Sidon and stay there. I have directed a widow there to supply you with food." (verse 17) So he went to Zarephath. When he came to the town gate, a widow was there gathering sticks. He called to her and asked, "Would you bring me a little water in a jar so I may have a drink?" ***As she was going to get it, he called,*** *"And bring me, please, a piece of bread."* (1 Kings 17:9–10)

The audacity of this guy! Okay, it's one thing to ask for a drink of water, but asking a poor widow for bread?

"As surely as the LORD your God lives," she replied, "I don't have any bread—only a handful of flour in a jar and a little olive oil in a jug. I am gathering a few sticks to take home and

make a meal for myself and my son, that we may eat it and die." Okay. So Elijah said, "I'm so sorry. I wouldn't think of taking a piece of bread from a starving widow and her son." NOT! This is what he said (verse 13): *"Don't be afraid. Go home and do as you have said. But first make a small loaf of bread for me from what you have and bring it to me, and then make something for yourself and your son."*

What? What kind of man was Elijah?—telling a widow to not only share her last morsel of food but to feed him first. Every warning bell in this woman's head should have been going off. But remember, God had told Elijah, "I have directed a widow to supply you with food."

I'm sure the widow didn't consciously realize she was being directed by God, but something inside told her to listen to Elijah—to put aside her fears and do something that seemed preposterous—even irresponsible. After all, she had more than herself to consider. She had a son at home who was starving to death. Sometimes God asks us to do something that seems absolutely irrational.

But what did the woman have to lose?

This was her last bite of food. It might keep her and her son alive another day. Maybe not even that. And it's important to note that Elijah didn't ask the woman to do this blindly. He told her what God's promise was (verse 14).

"For this is what the LORD, the God of Israel, says: 'The jar of flour will not be used up and the jug of oil will not run dry until the day the LORD sends rain on the land.'"

The widow faced a decision. Her choice was to believe what God was saying—or not. Faith is *hearing* what God says and believing it enough to *do* what He says. (verses 15-16)

"*She went away and did as Elijah had told her. So there was food every day for Elijah and for the woman and her family. For the jar of flour was not used up and the jug of oil did not run dry, in keeping with the word of the LORD spoken by Elijah."*

This widow had a choice to make. She could live in fear and hang on to what little bit she had, or she could believe the word of the Lord and share it with some guy she didn't even know.

What would have happened if this widow had hung on to that last little handful of meal? It would have been gone in a few bites, and she and her son would have died.

What Are We Hanging on To?

Elijah said, "Don't be afraid."

There's a lot of fear in America today, and with good reason, it would seem. People are concerned about their retirement, about terrorism, about an intrusive government. Some people are afraid of an economic collapse, so they stockpile food and supplies.

I'm not saying that we shouldn't save or invest or have a store of food on hand. We should do all of these. But what's our motive? Fear or faith? Is our trust in our retirement funds? Our savings account? The cellar where we have our hidden stockpile? God told the widow not to be afraid. To share what she had. Not to hang on to it.

And what happened? A miracle!

Matthew 6:19–21 (NIV) says: *"Do not store up for yourselves treasures on earth, where moths and vermin destroy, and where thieves break in and steal. But store up for yourselves treasures in Heaven, where moths and vermin do not destroy, and where thieves do not break in and steal. For where your treasure is, there your heart will be also."*

How do we store up treasures in heaven? By the way we treat people on earth.

I truly see nothing wrong with stockpiling supplies and food for a reasonable amount of time. There are any number of scenarios in which this would prove to be a wise decision.

I have a question though. Are you going to eat that food you've stored and watch your neighbors starve?

Is that what Jesus would do?

Now, if you're going to stockpile food so you'll have some to share with the hungry, I say, "Good for you." If you're going to stockpile food and hide it from your starving neighbors, that's not so good.

We *can* expect God to provide for us by a miracle if we open our hearts and share what we have with those who need it.

If we don't, we'll have to be content with what we can provide for ourselves, and no matter how well prepared we think we are, we can lose it all in an instant. If you don't believe that, study the Great Depression.

I believe we're facing some challenging times ahead. America is a lot like Israel was at the time of Elijah. We've set aside God and worshiped at the altar of materialism. Our greed and irresponsibility have brought us to a precarious place.

So what should our reaction be to this impending doom? Shake in our boots? No.

It's time to get close to God. Pray. Read the Bible. And then do what the Bible says. *"For I was hungry and you gave me something to eat. I was thirsty and you gave me something to drink. I was a stranger and you invited me in."*

This is no time to fear. It's a time to lay up treasures in heaven.

I think it's important to say that I'm primarily talking about bringing *believers* into your home.

Let's look at 1 Peter 4:9 again. *Practice hospitality to one another (those of the household of faith). Be hospitable, be a lover of strangers, with brotherly affection for the unknown guests, the foreigners, the poor, and all others who come your way who are of Christ's body . . .*

Some people are called to provide shelter for people with less-than-stellar backgrounds, but that's a special calling and one you need to consider carefully.

And in every circumstance, with believer or nonbeliever, you should follow the leading of the Holy Spirit—and be aware of the needs and safety of your children at all times.

It's time for another funny personal story. Elijah probably took some criticism for his interaction with the widow. My late husband could have lost his reputation also. I call this story "Who Moved the Swimming Pool?"

> Many years ago, my late husband and I were asked to minister for a weekend in a church in Tucson, Arizona. The pastor told us to check in at the Motel 8 on Miracle Mile and gave us the address. The church had an account with that motel, so the clerk knew Bill was a visiting preacher.
>
> We lived in a small town, so the first thing I always wanted to do when we hit the big city was shop! I left my husband in front of the TV and took off.
>
> I was known for two things back then: my love of shopping and my absolute lack of a sense of direction. Because of the latter, I took careful note of the Waffle House next to the motel.
>
> After several hours indulging in my favorite pastime, I headed back down Miracle Mile (which was much longer than a mile!) toward the Motel 8.

I saw my landmark—the Waffle House. There was the motel. Good! I didn't get lost.

I pulled in, grabbed my packages, and headed to room 104, wiping the Arizona sweat off my forehead, thinking about the swimming pool, which was right across from our room. I found the room, but something was wrong. Someone had moved the swimming pool! I checked my key: 104. I checked the door: 104. I looked again. No pool. What was going on here?

Oh, boy. Was it Motel 8 or Motel 6?

I went to the office. Sure enough. There was a Motel 6 on Miracle Mile. But there was also another Motel 8. It was a long street! The clerk thought the Motel 8 was probably where I was staying because it was next to a Waffle House. But maybe the Motel 6 was next to a Waffle House also. People in Tucson love their waffles!

She dialed the other Motel 8 and handed me the phone. The conversation went like this:

"Motel 8. How may I help you?"

"Yes. Could you tell me if Bill Thompson is registered there?"

"May I ask who's calling?"

"His wife."

A moment of silence.

"I'm sorry, but I can't give out that information."

Of course, the clerk had seen Bill check in with a young woman just a few hours earlier.

I meant to go to the office later and tell her

that the preacher in 104 was not having a tryst on the church's dime, but I forgot. I'm sure she told that story more than once. Just goes to show you, things aren't always what they seem.

Hospitality in the Church

Showing hospitality is not just for the individual. It's for the church. You've heard the old story about the man who was not allowed in a church because he wasn't properly dressed. Jesus met the man on the steps and told him not to worry—they wouldn't let Him in either. Unfortunately, that's probably more fact than fiction.

I wonder if Jesus would even be allowed to preach in many of the churches that carry His name today. He didn't fit into the religious template of His time. The Pharisees hated Him because He didn't follow "the rules" they laid on the shoulders of the people. My goodness, He even healed people on the Sabbath! He hadn't attended their schools, and his band of followers consisted mostly of ignorant fishermen and tax collectors! What could He or his uncouth, unschooled disciples offer these religious leaders?

I've known many people with a degree or two hanging around their necks who find it difficult to relate to the uneducated. Fortunately, knowledge and wisdom are not synonymous. Some of the wisest people I know have very little formal education, and being educated was definitely not a prerequisite to being called by God.

1 Corinthians 1:26–27 (NIV) puts it well. *Brothers and sisters, think of what you were when you were called. Not many of you were wise by human standards; not many were influen-*

tial; not many were of noble birth. But God chose the foolish things of the world to shame the wise; God chose the weak things of the world to shame the strong.

The Pharisees were the educated elite of their day, but it was they who persecuted the saints and condemned Jesus in an illegal trial.

The Scripture says not many wise by *human standards.* There was a hillbilly preacher from West Virginia that ministered at our church regularly who wouldn't have met the human standard for wisdom. His name was G. O. Wade. He said the initials stood for Going On. He wouldn't divulge what they really represented because his father named him when he was drunk! Once, in a moment of comradery, he told me his real name and made me promise never to tell. I kept his secret for decades, despite the nagging of my family. But now it's fallen into that hole where all the other things I've forgotten swim around aimlessly, so—no worries here G. O.! Your secret is still safe with me.

G. O. suffered from severe asthma. He was hospitalized so many times in his childhood, he wasn't able to go to school at all. As an adult, he lived in the hills of Kentucky and attended a snake-handling church. Yes. You read correctly! The church he attended took Luke 10:19 quite literally. *"Behold, I give unto you power to tread on serpents and scorpions, and over all the power of the enemy, and nothing shall by any means hurt you." (KJV)*

As G. O. grew in the Lord, he stopped handling snakes—for the most part. On occasion he would pick up one and preach to the congregation that loving their brother was a lot harder than handling a serpent. I don't know about that. Handling a snake would be pretty hard for me!

G. O. couldn't read or write, but he was one of the best preachers I have ever heard. He listened to the Bible on tape or his wife read it to him. His messages were so simple, they were profound. I can't say I remember many of the sermons I heard from ministers who visited our church in those years. But I still remember some that G. O. preached. To his credit, G. O. eventually earned his GED and studied at college level, but it was still the Holy Spirit that made his sermons what they were: gems of wisdom and grace. I'm certain that there were pastors who would not invite G. O. into their churches because of his lack of education. If so, they missed some wonderful wisdom that Jesus wanted to share with them.

Does your church embrace the stranger? Does it embrace the *least* of Jesus's brethren?

Hebrews 4:1 says, "Do not forget to entertain strangers, for by so doing some have unwittingly entertained angels.

I know a well-dressed perfectly coifed pastor's wife who has always had difficulty relating to people who don't look as if they just stepped out of a fashion magazine. One day she was telling me how a woman came to her church, and she was moved with compassion for the stranger. I was encouraged by this change of attitude. She said she went to greet the poorly dressed woman sitting alone on a pew. "I felt so sorry for her" she said. "I wanted to sit by her, so she wouldn't be alone—but she just smelled too bad."

I hope *that* woman wasn't an angel!

That pastor's wife was worried about physical smell, but many congregations reject people whose lives don't smell squeaky clean. I like this message I saw on a church sign: "Sinners welcome here." I'm glad to hear it. Why? Because I'm a sinner!

What kind of people are welcome at your church? Divorced people? Convicted child abusers?

A young man in the town we once lived in spent five years in prison for sexually abusing a minor. He was a Christian who had been abused himself. My husband wrote to him every week while he was in prison. He went to see him several times. When the young man got out of prison, he was ostracized by the church. He had to register as a sex offender, so he couldn't get a job. If his wife hadn't stood by him, I think he would have committed suicide. I hated what that man did, but I didn't hate it nearly as much as he hated it. He was completely broken, and he didn't know where to turn for help.

Would you sit by that man in church? What about a gay or lesbian couple? A transgender?

I'm not saying you have to approve of what people do. But, if you want to please God, you do have to love them. Shouldn't anyone be welcome to hear the Word of God?

I think there's a difference between allowing people to attend a church and actually welcoming them. If you take a close look at Jesus's ministry, you find the only people he shunned were the religious leaders of His day.

Where's the diversity in our churches? In my opinion, if our congregants are all of one color, one socioeconomic strata, and one political party, we have some work to do.

If your church isn't as welcoming as you'd like, maybe you could take it upon yourself to set an example of Christ's love. Find someone who looks uncomfortable and engage them. If you're just performing a duty, they'll know it, and you'll make them feel more uncomfortable. Do it from the heart, and they'll recognize your sincerity and likely respond.

One of the loneliest times for many people is right after church when they hear people talking about where they're going for lunch. No one wants to go to a restaurant by themselves. I've been in that position. It's hard to walk out the door of the church knowing you're going home to an empty house and a tuna fish sandwich. It's good to be on the watch for people who live alone. Invite them to have lunch with you. You have no idea what it will mean to them.

What about America? Are We a Welcoming Nation?

Racist is a term that should not be wielded thoughtlessly. It's one of the greatest insults that can be given. But in America, we have a sad history of thinking people of color less valuable for the hue of their skin.

The church we pastored in Clifton, Arizona, was about 99 percent Mexican-American when we started it, and about 80 percent when we resigned fourteen years later. Most of the people were second- or third-generation American citizens. We had a wonderful congregation full of loving people. Racial prejudice was not an issue in our small town. We didn't think in terms of race when we considered one another—unless we were having a potluck—then we sure as heck expected authentic Mexican food!

One time, my husband and I invited a beautiful young couple of Mexican descent to take a trip to Texas with us. I have to interject that these people were better dressed than we were, and they spoke very good English, with only a trace of an accent.

We stopped at one of those little local cafes because they usually have great food. It was off-peak hours, and the place wasn't very busy. There were two or three tables besides ours. The waitress was very congenial—with the other customers. She wasn't busy, but it took forever for her to bring our menus. We were chatting, so we didn't pay much attention when she took even longer to take our orders. We still weren't really getting that there was something weird here until we got our plates and I asked for some condiment that wasn't on the table.

Her response was: "Some people wouldn't be happy if you hung them with a new rope." What? Because we didn't even *think* in terms of race with the young couple, we were still confused, until we noticed the look she was giving them, and, of course, she considered us beneath her because we would associate with Mexicans. I wonder what that woman will say when she stands in the judgment and Jesus tells her she told Him He wouldn't be satisfied if someone hung Him with a new rope. Wouldn't want to be in her shoes on that one!

And if the woman wouldn't make these lovely people welcome in her workplace, she certainly wouldn't have made them welcome in her home.

Once, while attending a church in the Deep South, I actually witnessed a lay minister stand and say that God made black people to be slaves and servants. I couldn't believe my ears. I'm ashamed of myself for not walking out of that service, even though I was attending with someone else and didn't have my own transportation. Today, I wouldn't hesitate. I'd walk home.

Most of us would find such an assertion reprehensible, but all racism is not so easy to spot. There's a lot of talk today of white supremacy. Most of us who are white loudly condemn people who tout this inexcusable belief, but could there be just a smidge of it staining our lily-white hands? How do you feel when you see a mixed-race couple? Does it bother you?

Would you be upset if your child wanted to marry someone of a different race? Even if he or she were a believer?

I'm proud to say that my family is about as mixed up as you can get. The only race unrepresented is Asian. But we're not done with marriages yet, so there's still hope!

Prejudice means to pre-judge. Do we judge people before we get to know them? Do we even try to get to know those who are dissimilar to us? Are all our friends one skin color?—or do we have a little variation of shades on our buddy palettes? When we get to know those of a different race or culture better, the differences tend to fade into the background.

What about Immigrants?

Immigration is a hot topic these days. I know there are valid arguments for and against our present immigration policies. I lived in Arizona for many years, so I'm not without some personal knowledge of both sides of the issues on our southern border.

Believe me, I have no intention of entering the morass of politics in this book. What I want to talk about is the *heart* of our country.

You've heard it before: America is a nation of immigrants. Buy one of those handy-dandy new DNA kits, and you'll discover that, unless you're Native American, your relatives came from somewhere besides the good ol' US of A.

The poem written by Emma Lazarus embodies the open-armed attitude our country once had.

Give me your tired, your poor,
Your huddled masses, yearning to breathe free,
The wretched refuse of your teeming shore,
Send these, the homeless, tempest tost to me,
I lift my lamp beside the golden door.

But our collective attitude has changed. We're not quite as welcoming to the world's "huddled masses" as we were at one time. I know there are legitimate reasons to limit immigration, to vet people who enter our country. What I am concerned about is the attitude I see in our country toward the misplaced peoples of the world. I worry about the *heart* of America toward *the stranger*. For the most part, it's not one of compassion.

Perhaps it's because we've been overexposed that we've lost our sensitivity to suffering peoples. We're no longer moved by pictures of starving children covered with flies. We don't feel the pain of people fleeing their homes for their lives—especially people who don't look like us.

We may not be able to help everyone. We may have to close our doors at times, for the good of our own people—but we should never close our hearts. And we should treat the people who do come to America seeking refuge with kindness.

God spoke to it in Exodus 22:21: *"Do not mistreat or oppress a foreigner, for you were foreigners in Egypt."*

Much of the diatribe—even among Christians—is mean-spirited. Especially toward immigrants from Middle-Eastern countries. Not long ago, I was visiting some friends. A Muslim family had just moved into their neighborhood. I was shocked at the way my Christian friends talked about their new neighbors. They wouldn't even allow their children to play with the Muslim children. It was as though the enemy had moved in next door, and my friends were gearing up for war. Where was the "love your neighbor as yourself" in that situation?

Is America in the "goat" line these days when it comes to entertaining strangers? I hope not. But I think Matthew 25 can be applied to nations as well as individuals. In fact, the passage actually says, "All the *nations* will be gathered before

Him, and He will separate them one from another, as a shepherd divides his sheep from the goats."

Nations are made up of people. So the "whatever you did for one of the least of these you did for me" test of Matthew 25:40 would seem to apply to us as a nation as well as individuals.

Are we, as Americans, mistreating the son of faithful Abraham? What do you feel when you look at a dark-skinned young man of obvious Middle-Eastern descent? Suspicion? Fear? Loathing?

God brought something to my attention that has changed my perception considerably. When I see such a person now, I see Abraham. I hear Abraham's cry for his son Ishmael.

God had promised Abraham that his descendants would be as innumerable as the stars in the sky or the sands on the shore. He promised that Abraham's seed would be a blessing to the whole world. Of course, ultimately, that seed is referring to Jesus, who became the propitiation for the sins of the world. But that all had to start with one child—and Abraham's wife was barren.

It was a common practice at that time for a barren woman to send her husband to sleep with her servant in order to produce an heir. The barren woman would be the legal mother. It was the ancient equivalent of modern-day surrogacy.

So Sarah sent Abraham to her handmaiden's bed. Ishmael was born of Hagar, Sarah's Egyptian slave.

But it was God's plan that Sarah bear the child that would start this whole journey to the cross.

As noted in Genesis 17:16, God told Abraham He was going to give him a son by Sarah. This should have been wonderful news, right? But Abraham laughed. It was hard for him to believe, since Sarah had already gone through menopause. Abraham said to God, "If only Ishmael might live under Your blessing!"

It appears to me Abraham was asking God to choose the son he already had. He loved Ishmael. Maybe he had some sense of what would happen if Sarah had a son, fearing Ishmael would be displaced.

God didn't reprove Abraham. Instead, He said, *"And as for Ishmael, I have heard you. Behold, I have blessed him, and will make him fruitful, and will multiply him exceedingly. He shall beget twelve princes, and I will make him a great nation" (verse 20).*

Menopause or no, Sarah got pregnant and had the son God promised. After Isaac was born, things got worse. When Ishmael mocked Isaac, Sarah demanded that Abraham send Hagar and Ishmael away.

Abraham was upset. He loved both of his sons. But God gave him what might seem like a strange command. He said not to be distressed about Ishmael and his mother—and to do what Sarah said. He promised Abraham he would make Ishmael a nation also, because he was Abraham's offspring.

The next morning Abraham took a skin of water and some food and placed it on Hagar's shoulders and sent her off with their son. Seems kind of harsh, doesn't it? As if Abraham didn't care that much about Ishmael. But I don't believe that was true. I see this as an experience similar to when God told Abraham to offer Isaac as a sacrifice on the mountain. Abraham obeyed God in both instances and committed his sons to God's keeping, even though the commands seemed reprehensible.

Hagar and Ishmael ran out of water, so she left her child

under a bush and went a bowshot away because she didn't want to watch him die. She was crying when she heard a voice tell her not to be afraid—God had heard the boy's cries. Her son was not going to die. God was going to make him into a great nation. God directed her vision to a well of water, where she filled the skin and took it back to Ishmael. God protected the son of the patriarch.

The Scripture tells us that *"God was with the boy as he grew up. He lived in the desert and became an archer"* (Genesis 21:20).

I think some Christians might be surprised at that statement. It's easy to think of Ishmael as Isaac's nemesis because of the conflict still raging between their respective descendants. But God was with Ishmael because he was Abraham's son, and I don't believe God has forgotten His promise to Abraham—in fact, I think there's evidence to the contrary.

God Hasn't Forgotten His Promise to Abraham

Something phenomenal is happening in these latter days that, I believe, is an answer to Abraham's prayers for his older son. When I was researching for an article I was writing for a missionary magazine several years ago, I was surprised to find testimonies that thousands of Muslims have come to Christ through dreams in which they see Jesus, his hands outstretched. I invite you to Google it. You'll find testimony after testimony of Muslims from Middle-Eastern countries and around the world that have had very similar dreams and through them have come to know Christ as their Savior.

Could it be God is keeping His promise to Abraham by speaking to the children of Ishmael through dreams of the risen Christ?

In his book *Dreams and Visions: Is Jesus Awakening the Muslim World?* Tom Doyle documents many such conversions. Doyle says "Could it be that the real story about Muslims today is not global terrorism? Could it be the real story about Muslims is that Jesus is reaching out to them with His offer of eternal life earned by His death on the cross and resurrection from the dead?"

Doyle goes on to say, "I believe Islamic terrorism is Satan's attempt to keep the gospel message away from Muslims. The enemy thinks that if he can make the rest of us afraid of Muslims or make us hate them, then he can short-circuit Jesus's church from reaching Muslims. But that isn't working. Jesus has stepped in and is opening Muslim hearts Himself."

This is a profound statement. *Who* is trying to make us fear or hate Muslims? Satan! Every time we see a son of Ishmael, we should be reminded of the faithfulness of our loving God to the seed of Abraham. And we should be filled with love and compassion and a deep desire to see him come to Christ.

Sheltering Jews During WWII

Some of the greatest acts of hospitality were extended to Jews during WWII. We've all seen the movies, read the books, heard the testimonies. Can you imagine making the choice to shelter a Jewish family at the risk of your own?

In her book *The Hiding Place,* Corrie ten Boom tells how she and her family, seeing their Jewish friends and neighbors facing arrest and probable death if caught by the Nazis, became involved in an underground endeavor to provide refuge for a multitude of God's chosen people.

They obtained ration cards and false identity papers, and turned their 150-year-old house, affectionately dubbed the *Beje,* into a refuge, shuttling endangered Jewish men, women, and children to safer accommodations. The *Beje* was half a block from the main police headquarters. After many close calls, underground carpenters and craftsmen created a wall with a secret opening in Corrie's bedroom that perfectly matched the patina of the more-than-a-century-old room. Behind it was a narrow space that could shelter several people should the house be raided.

Because they couldn't be depended on to keep quiet, sheltering babies posed a greater risk. In her book, Corrie tells of the family's concern for a mother and her two-week-old baby that were staying with them until a safer place could be found. Father ten Boom was a watchmaker, and the bottom floor of the *Beje* was his shop. He had taught Corrie his craft, and she had become the first female watchmaker in Poland. Corrie and her sister, Betsie, were what would have been called "old maids" in that time—unlikely to be suspected of such surreptitious activity. But her concern for the mother and child staying in the family home, and the other "guests" that would be endangered should the child cry at an inopportune time, made her take a chance when a pastor she knew brought a watch into the shop for repair.

The clergyman pastored a church in a small town outside of the city and lived in a house set back from the street in a large wooded area. The perfect place to hide a wailing infant. Corrie invited the pastor upstairs to the dining room and asked him if he would be willing to welcome the Jewish mother and her baby into his home. She told him that the mother and child would almost certainly be arrested otherwise. Corrie was exposing her clandestine activity, endangering her own safety and that of her family, in the hope of touching this pastor's heart.

The man replied, "Miss ten Boom. I do hope you're not involved with any of this illegal concealment and undercover business. It's just not safe! Think of your father! And your sister—she's never been strong!"

Corrie asked the pastor to wait and ran upstairs and brought the baby down. She pulled back the blanket so the pastor could look at the baby's face. Corrie said she could see the compassion and fear struggle in his visage. After a moment the man said, "No. Definitely not. We could lose our lives for that Jewish child!"

At that moment, Corrie's father appeared. The wizened old man took the baby in his arms and said to the pastor,

"You say we could lose our lives for this child. I would consider that the greatest honor that could come to my family." Angry, the pastor turned and left.

Knowing they *had* to move the mother and child now, they sent them to another safe house. The place was raided. The mother and child and the people who had protected them were taken, and Corrie's family never found out what became of them.

I know it was a difficult decision, but I can't imagine how this *man of God* was able to live with it. And, of course, when he stands at the judgment seat of Christ, he will realize that he had turned away Christ Himself when he turned away that child.

Eventually, someone betrayed the ten Boom family, and they were arrested. While at the Gestapo headquarters, the chief interrogator looked at Corrie's father, who was an elderly white-haired old gentleman who could hardly stand on his own. According to the book, he said, "I'd like to send you home, old fellow. I'll take your word that you won't cause any more trouble."

Casper ten Boom straightened his shoulders and gently told the man, "If I go home today, tomorrow I will open my door again to any man in need who knocks." The men were sent to different camps than the women. After the war, Corrie learned that her father had died ten days after he entered a concentration camp.

I'm writing this with tears in my eyes. What courage! Could I have such courage in the face of death? Only by the grace of God.

"Greater love hath no man than this, that a man lay down his life for his friends" (John 15:13 KJV).

It is estimated that hundreds of thousands of Polish Christians hid or aided Jews during WWII. Thousands have been awarded the title of *Righteous among the Nations* by the State of Israel for saving Jews from extermination during this terrible atrocity. But that honor was insignificant next to the words they must have heard from Jesus when they stood at the judgment: "I was a stranger and you took me in."

When asked which was the greatest commandment, Jesus said, "Love the Lord your God with all your heart and with all your soul and with all your mind and with all your strength. The second is this: Love your neighbor as yourself. There is no commandment greater than these" (Mark 12:29–31 KJV).

We may never be called upon to make such sacrifices as Corrie ten Boom and her family made, but every cup of water, every bite of food, every blanket or piece of clothing we give to those in need we are giving to Jesus.

Taking Hospitality to the Streets

Perhaps you're unable to invite people to your home. You would like to, but your spouse wouldn't approve. Or maybe you're afraid. I understand. Don't be disheartened. There is much you can do outside of your home, but I hope whatever you choose to do involves actually engaging with the people you're trying to help.

Donating to a food bank is commendable. But . . . have you ever done a food drive? Usually the collection consists of mountains of canned green beans and piles of Hamburger Helper. I always wonder why people donate Hamburger Helper to people with no hamburger. I'm not knocking food drives. They're necessary, but it's far too easy to drop off the box of unwanted cans we've cleaned out of our cupboards and think we've done our duty.

I wonder what the reward in heaven is for giving Jesus a can of cold green beans? Sorry for the sarcasm! Please give to your local food bank. We all should. But don't miss out on the joy of engaging people in need.

Susanne, a dear friend of mine, keeps a sealed tub in the trunk of her car filled with bags of food and necessary items. When she sees someone on the street that needs help, she gets out of her car, gives the person the bag, then offers to buy the person a hot meal. She sits down and engages the person in conversation. Asks what other needs she has that Susanne might be able to meet. She shows interest in the person as an individual. You would be surprised at the fascinating people you meet on the streets. Every human being is made in God's image and deserves to be treated with respect.

One of Susanne's recommendations is to give your gifts in black garbage bags. Pretty packages invite theft.

A few years ago there was much criticism in the media of a homeless man who appeared barefoot on the street the day after a first responder took him to a shoe store and bought him a pair of sneakers that cost one hundred dollars. The reporters assumed the man didn't wear the new shoes because he was trying to scam someone for another pair, or he sold them for booze. The homeless man responded that if he wore the shoes, someone might attack him and take them. People have been killed for less. It may have been wiser for the good Samaritan to take the man to a thrift store and buy him a sturdy, comfortable pair of shoes that would not draw attention.

What about giving to people begging on the street? Many people worry that their money will be used at the corner liquor store. I don't worry too much about that. If I have no food to give, I give them the money. You may disagree with me—and I may be wrong—but I'd rather err on the side of compassion than assume the person is lying about being hungry. The same is true of people who say they're out of gas, or their car broke down and they need to catch a bus home. Rarely do I refuse to give, even if I have doubts about their stories. I just leave it in God's hands and pray the people do what they said they were going to do with my money.

Another great street ministry is handing out blankets and coats. I hate being cold more than almost anything. I live in northern Nevada, but I'm an Arizona transplant. I have to admit that I sometimes sit at my window in my warm house looking out at the snow and ice praying for people who are cold. How terrible is that? I don't seem to think about people without warm clothing and shelter until the cold is upon us. Some things take a little planning and preparation. I feel like the person addressed in this Scripture:

> *If a brother or sister is naked or destitute of daily food and one of you says to them, "Depart in peace, be warmed and filled," but you do not give them the things which are needed for the body, what does it profit?* (James 2:15–16 NKJ)

I'm fairly certain that, given a choice, a person exposed to the elements would rather have a coat than my prayers. With the Lord's help, I plan to do better on that front in the future.

While I was writing this book, a dear friend of mine died of a heart attack. It was a shock to everyone. His name was Randy Clonts. Randy was a wonderful example of someone taking the love of Christ to the streets. He had a vision for rural America.

Like many small towns the greatest complaint among the young was that there was nothing to do—except of course, cruise Main Street—literally. That was the name of the street where cars loaded with teens moved at the speed of a terrapin, honking their horns and calling out to their friends leaning against the old store buildings. When other people saw a nuisance, and complained at city council meetings and from their comfortable church pews, Randy saw an opportunity.

My friend was not a man of means—far from it—but he

was a visionary, and somehow he managed to purchase an old store building right in the middle of this stretch of cars and kids. He called it *The Stir*. The name had a double meaning. He and his beautiful wife served gallons of coffee and stirred young souls toward Christ.

Randy didn't care what the kids looked like, if they attended church regularly—or at all. Some came for the free food and the bands. Some for the pinball machines and the pool table, or the chance to spy out the local lookers. But what they all received was unconditional love. Randy *loved* these kids. My own two sons were greatly affected by that love. They've shed buckets of tears the last few days. Randy was buried just two days ago.

One of the young men who was greatly affected was a boy who went by the name of Damien. He posted his story on Facebook. The family read it at the funeral, and I'm going to share some of it with you here.

> It is with great, great sadness that I just learned that someone I love deeply has just passed from this world. Randy Clonts was my longest held friend, and it is very hard on me to see him leave us. It is not without a great many tears in my house from all of us. I can barely keep composure to write this. Randy passed away on Friday, March 2—my birthday. The timing is very fitting to me, and I'll honor his memory in telling you why.
>
> When I was an atheist teenager with a huge chip on my shoulder living in Safford Arizona, a place with nothing to do at all, there was a little place called The Stir. It was a place started by

a wonderful, compassionate man named Randy Clonts for the sole purpose of giving kids a place to go to do something besides get involved in drugs, crime and other things that would lead conflicted kids down the wrong path.

I would go and play pool and try to look menacing, but Randy would come up to me and talk with me like I was human, ignoring my posturing. He would tell me how much God loved me and was bigger than all my issues. No matter how many walls I put up, he would ignore them and sit right by me and ask if I wanted to talk. He would always listen with compassion and put his hand on my shoulder and empathize with me. I couldn't help but love him.

One day I came in on my birthday and he and his equally amazing wife, **Diana, were waiting with presents and a cake to celebrate my birthday. Nobody else in Safford seemed to care that this nearly homeless teenager was turning eighteen, but they made a big deal out of it and made me feel special**, like they always did. He was instrumental in me realizing that God was here and could be found in the hearts of those who love Him, people like Randy. He had so much God that He came out of his pores and rested on the shoulder of a confused seventeen-year-old boy.

Since those days God showed Himself to me, and I've spent my life falling in love with Him personally. When I met the woman I wanted to

> marry, Randy helped show her that God was real as well, and so when i asked Randy to perform the ceremony, of course, he happily obliged. I wouldn't have had it any other way. Randy, my brother, my mentor, my cherished ambassador to the Heavens...with many hot tears I say good night my sweet friend, and I'll see you in the morning. Until then, we'll all miss you so very much.

What greater honor could a man be given? When Randy entered the gates of Heaven a few days ago, I believe Jesus greeted him with theses words: *I was a stranger, and you took me in. Well done, my good and faithful servant.*

Give Without Grumbling

It's important that we have the right attitude when entertaining strangers. I'll have to admit: I've fallen into a bad attitude more a few times when I could barely get the sheets washed between guests. And in all honesty, sometimes it *was* a little too much. But it was nothing compared to what Corrie ten Boon and her family went through. I'm certain they often felt it was more than they could handle. The following Scripture tells us how we should offer hospitality.

Offer hospitality to one another without grumbling. Each of you should use whatever gift you have received to serve others, as faithful stewards of God's grace in its various forms. (I Peter 4:9–10 NIV)

We are to use the gifts we have received to *serve others.* We are a blessed people. We have material gifts: houses, cars, food, money. And we have spiritual gifts.

There are different kinds of gifts, but the same Spirit distributes them. There are different kinds of service, but the same Lord. There are different kinds of working, but in all of them and in everyone it is the same God at work. Now to each one the manifestation of the Spirit is given for the common good. (1 Corinthians 12:4–7 NIV)

What was that? *For the common good.* Our gifts weren't given to us simply for our own benefit. They were given to us for the *common* good. I have to confess something here.

I am a selfish person. I'm not trying to be humble. I battle with selfishness all the time. I don't want to be that way, but I am. It takes a concerted effort to overcome selfishness. It's work, and to be honest, sometimes I just don't want to make the effort.

My present husband is one of the most unselfish people I know. He has the heart of a servant. It just seems to come naturally to him. Maybe I'm selfish because I was the baby of the family. I'm not sure, but it's a constant battle for me to put others before myself, and I don't always do a good job of it. Sometimes I have to make myself do the unselfish thing, even if I don't feel it emotionally. It's not our feelings that count. It's our actions. Remember, the Bible tells us we'll be judged for the *deeds* done in the body. Don't grumble (that's an action) when you do something for the needy. Remember who you're really doing it for—Jesus. After you've done it, you're going to feel better, and it will be easier the next time.

It's important to teach our children not to grumble. I've stayed in homes where the children didn't even try to hide their bad attitudes. They didn't want to give up their space, and they wanted me to know it. I've often wondered how some of those children have fared in adulthood. Did they grow up to be generous adults? I hope so, but it probably took a few hard knocks for them to get there.

I promised a word from each of my four children about how their adult lives have reflected their childhood experiences with hospitality. Josh is eight years younger than his older brother and twelve years younger than his oldest sister. He experienced many of the things I've talked about in this book as a little boy. Here's what he had to say on the matter.

Let's face it. Children are not known for their selflessness. Absent any outside influence, the words *mine* and *no* are among the first that we utter. And the inclination to be selfish doesn't really go away when we become an adult. It's our awareness that changes. And when you're aware of how little thought and consideration you demonstrate outside of yourself, it produces conviction, and conviction leads to action, and action leads to change.

I didn't necessarily want to give up my bed to accommodate our guests. But, even as a small child who was otherwise unaware of what was happening around him, somehow I knew that it was a good thing. The benefit of growing up in this kind of environment is that it provided my life with a template. As an adult, when I feel "put out" **at the thought of giving up my personal space, it's my past that reminds me of who I want to be in the present.**

What Now?

Want to stay out of the goat lane? It's not my purpose to pile on guilt. It's my purpose to help us get into the right line on Judgment Day. I don't want Jesus to say to me, "I was a stranger and you took me *not* in." I know there are many of us that want to do the right thing but just don't know where to start. What about that youth group visiting your church that needs housing? Or itinerate missionaries or ministers?

I think it's sad that we tend to put visiting ministers in motels now. I know most ministers would rather not stay in the pastor's home. When we were traveling evangelists, I always enjoyed staying in a motel when the opportunity was given. But I remember very little about the motels we stayed in and a great deal about the families we stayed with. Some of my dearest friends are people who welcomed our family into their homes while we were ministering in their churches. It takes little effort to send someone to the local Comfort Inn, but it can be a great joy to share your home with God's people. That's how it was done in the Bible. And, yes, they did have inns back then.

I suspect someday this biblical principle will be restored to the church out of necessity. Persecution drove the early believers from their homes. We may be required to seek refuge with one another like the Jews did during WWII. Who knows? But for now, why not try to crack the door just a little?

Tips and Testimonies

What's the first sense that is engaged when you enter a home—or any enclosed space, for that matter? You got it! Smell. Unfortunately, we tend to become nose-blind to our own domiciles. They say if you want to sell your house, bake cookies just before you show it. But of course, cookies (check out my recipe for Cowboy Cookies in the Cooking for Company cookbook) may not be on the menu, so I'll share some other tips with you.

I wish I could say there was an easier way, but the most important thing you can do to eliminate odors is give your place a thorough cleaning. Sorry. Believe me, I wish there was another way. I have more important things to do than clean house. We don't mind our own dirt, but we really don't like other people's. I've stayed in many homes, so I'm talking from personal experience.

I didn't mind clutter at all, but if I went into the bathroom and found feces on the toilet, toothpaste in the sink, and hair in the bathtub, I got a little queasy. And don't forget the bathroom rug! And is it time to replace that moldy plastic shower curtain? One more thing: when you pull the guest towels from the linen closet, make sure they smell fresh. If you don't have time to rewash them, put them in the dryer with a fabric softener sheet (that goes for sheets, pillowcases, and blankets also). And you might want to tell your family not to use them.

My kids knew that touching the guest towels before company came could result in loss of a limb. I read somewhere that a woman put this sign on the guest towel rack: DO NOT USE THESE TOWELS! Only problem was she forgot to take the sign down before the guests arrived, which is why I preferred oral threats.

Once we were invited to stay with a pastor's family while we ministered at their church. They were a beautiful couple with two beautiful kids and a beautiful home, but we walked in the house to the smell of several days' dishes in the sink (and on the counters—the sink couldn't hold them), clothes needing folding on the couch, and general disarray. Remember, I told you clutter doesn't bother me (ask my husband), so I was trying to stay positive about what we were going to find in the bedroom. Nothing could have prepared me.

The sheets were so filthy, I thought there might be creatures living under the covers. It was their son's room, and I don't think the sheets had been washed since he graduated from the crib (he was a teenager). Slight exaggeration, but they were dirtier than any sheets I've ever seen. There was no way my husband and I could sleep on them, so we slept on top of the covers. At least we couldn't *see* the dirt.

But that's not the whole story. It was a waterbed, and we had no covers over us. That night I dreamed I was on a boat in a storm, the spray blowing in my face. I was afraid the ship was going to sink, and I was going to a watery grave (no exaggeration!).

I have to say something about that young man though. He was as gracious as he could be about giving up his room.

The family was wonderful and became great friends of ours. We stayed with them many times through the years, and I don't remember sleeping on sheets like that again. I'm sure the boy's mother asked him if his sheets were clean, and he said, "Yup." So another lesson—always check your kids' rooms yourself if you're going to put guests in them.

I like to clean with orange cleaners. They leave a "I just cleaned the house" aroma that's not overwhelming. I also love scented candles, but some people can't tolerate them, so I would avoid them unless you know the guests. And it always helps to give the house an airing.

Clean It and Forget It

Well, your guests have arrived to your freshly cleaned house! Now what? Don't worry about it anymore. They have come to see you, not your house. Sure, pick up, wash dishes, do what you have to do, but don't obsess about the house. If you go around picking up after people every moment, they become uncomfortable. Relax!

Give your guests space. Especially, people who are on the road frequently. Don't feel as if you have to entertain them every minute. Tell them when meals will be served and what's in the refrigerator, then leave them alone for awhile.

Temporary Means Temporary

Be hospitable, loving, and kind, but don't let people take advantage of the situation. It's not good for them or you. We all do better when we know the boundaries. So, if you've offered temporary housing for someone in need, the key word is *temporary*. Talk to them about their plans, their needs, then follow up with conversations about what they're doing to get to their goals. Don't wait until the day they're supposed to move out to mention it.

If your guests are staying for a while, set expectations up front. Always speak kindly, and be careful how you phrase your requests. I like to couch things this way: "We're so glad to have you with us (we are). I'm sure you're wondering what you can do to help, so I'd like to suggest . . ." then show them where to find things, and make sure they know how to operate your appliances.

I remember staying in someone's home when I was in my early twenties. I really wanted to help, but I had no idea what to do. The house was beautiful, and I was nervous about doing something wrong, so I did nothing. I was very uncomfortable, and when my hostess finally gave me some chores to do, I was embarrassed that she had to ask. Some people really aren't good about just looking around, seeing what needs to be done, and diving in.

We had a young man staying with us once who left his

beard cuttings in the sink of the only bathroom. When my husband talked to him about it, he was offended and left. A few words about cleaning up after yourself in the beginning would probably have saved some hard feelings.

On my blog, my middle daughter addressed the subject of being taken advantage of, so here's a portion of her article.

> When I grew older and moved to a big city, my mom would call me and say, "We're bringing a youth group to town, and they need a place to stay. I'd just say, "How many?" and we'd make it happen, even though I lived in a one-bedroom apartment. I remember waking up one morning to go to the kitchen and stepping over lines of bodies lying on my living room floor.
>
> That sense of hospitality was instilled in us at a young age. As an adult, it's sometimes gotten me into a little trouble because I want to help everyone. I've had to learn when it's being hospitable and when it's being taken advantage of. I have to say, it took me years to find a happy medium.
>
> Opening yourself to help and serve others is very gratifying. It seems these days we are all so concerned with what we have going on—we forget we have a lot to give.

Sara is generous to a fault—literally. I'm glad she's found some balance, but I wouldn't change her for anything!

The Entertainer in the Family

Rebecca, my oldest daughter, is the party-thrower in the family. I changed sheets and cooked and provided a place for people to stay, but I seldom threw parties. Rebecca learned that from our dear friend, Lupe Urrea. Like Randy, Lupe went home to be with Jesus while I was writing this book. Two dear friends of mine from the same town, who were awesome servants of God. Both of them followed the principles of Matthew 25 better than I ever have. They are with Jesus, but I miss them so very much. If God throws parties, He's got the girl to do it! Lupe was the best hostess I have ever met, and she taught my daughter well.

Here are Rebecca's words about how the hospitality in our home affected her as an adult, and some tips on how to entertain guests.

> Some of my fondest memories were when ministers would come to our church to speak, and my parents would have them stay in our home rather then a hotel. Most of them had children, and to this day I have many special friendships with people across the United States because my parents showed them hospitality.
>
> I remember some funny stories and some not so funny. One not so funny was when a very dignified elderly preacher was staying with us, and

I walked in on him sitting on the toilet (hey, not my fault he didn't know how to lock a door!).

Another time I walked in to find a preacher and his family had brought a little black-and-white TV with them and were watching it very quietly in the room. If you don't know yet, we weren't raised with a TV, only getting one when I was a teenager. And we had *no* cable because cable was from the *pits of hell* **lol! We were finally allowed to watch old Disney movies like** *Old Yeller* and *The Apple Dumpling Gang* on a VCR years later. So, you can imagine my horror in finding a preacher watching *Green Acres* on a television in Brother Bill's house.

Wait.

What?!!!

I was so scared for their souls. I think they survived the fire and brimstone, last time I heard. (Rolls eyes)

If you're wondering how we fed all these people and where they slept, well, somehow it all worked out. For instance, one night every bed and piece of floor was occupied, so after wandering through the house looking for a place to sleep, I ended up making a bed in the bathtub. I loved it! What fun! It didn't last long, though, as in the middle of the night a guest heard nature calling, and I got bumped to the hallway floor. I think we had enough beds, blankets, and pillows in our home to fill the Arizona desert.

On a more serious note, if you are one who

is interested in opening up your life and home to others in your community, then you might be interested in a few tips I have learned from my parents.

One thing I learned from their example was not to be afraid to talk to people, to engage.

When we host parties, Bible studies, sing-offs, karaoke, etc. in our home, people ask me how I am able to keep the guests so engaged. It's actually not that hard.

First of all, you need enough places to sit. Ask everyone to bring a chair of some sort if you don't have enough. You don't need a bunch of Pinterest-worthy table decorations. To be honest, if everyone is having a good time, they won't notice what they're eating off of.

Second, **if you're just having people over for the evening, have everyone bring their favorite dish, which takes away the burden of paying for everything yourself.**

Next, have music on at all times. You can do that simply with your smartphone or TV. Pandora has all types of music. Music is vital to hospitality, which brings me to the next tip. If the people you're inviting over play an instrument or sing, have them bring some music to share. That's always fun and keeps things moving, without anyone getting bored. This is something that I experienced as a child that has become a norm in my own household.

The most important tip I could give you in

hosting people in your home is learn to be a listener. While everyone is having a good time, walk around asking people if they need anything. Ask how they're doing. Engage! This is vital. To show people you care and enjoy them being there, you want to ask them questions about themselves. Ask where they work, if they like their job, if they have any hobbies, etc. You'll be surprised at how much people like to talk about themselves :). I personally love hearing people's histories.

Last, but not least, **the grim reality is some people don't want to invite people into their home because of fear for their kids' personal safety. This is a valid concern. As a preacher's kid I've seen and heard of situations that have brought pain to families. Let me give you some advice:**

First of all, it's your job to protect your kids and your belongings. As far as important belongings go, lock them up. No one will ever know you did it.

When it comes to your family, you can either have a spot for the kids to play together and pop in often to see how they're doing, or you can have the kids help with hosting, passing out food and drinks, then direct them to a craft spot where you can keep an eye on them.

I personally would not recommend allowing a child to be alone in a room with another adult. Being smart while being hospitable will save you a lot of trouble.

> Overall, hospitality has been beneficial in my life and my siblings' lives. Because of the generosity of my parents, I have dozens of very special relationships.
>
> Hospitality is a lost art and blessing that needs to be introduced back into our lives.

I didn't know about the secreted television until I read Rebecca's piece. I would have watched it with them! One thing that Rebecca didn't mention is that she watches for people in her church and neighborhood who are alone and often invites them to her home when she has a gathering. She's a wonderful hostess and a wonderful person. I'm very proud of her.

Wrapping It Up

I hope that you've found this book helpful. As I've grown older (not old!), I've begun thinking more about death and what comes after. I don't want to meet my God empty-handed. When I stand before the judgment seat of Christ, as all believers will, I want more than anything for Him to say to me what is written in Matthew 25:34–35. *"Come you who are blessed of my Father; take your inheritance, the kingdom prepared for you since the creation of the world. For I was hungry and you gave me something to eat. I was thirsty and you gave me something to drink. I was a stranger and you invited me in. I needed clothes and you clothed me. I was sick and you looked after me. I was in prison and you came to visit me."* (NIV)

This life is all we have to garner rewards in heaven. Remember what Jesus said in verse 40 of the same chapter: "Truly I tell you, whatever you did for one of the least of these brothers and sisters of mine, you did for me." Let's look for Jesus in the face of the needy, the lonely, the hungry—the stranger. When we stand before Him, we'll be glad we did.

Read on for some great recipes to help you feed all the wonderful people you're going to invite into your home.

Cooking for Company

All of my recipes with green chili are best with fresh Hatch N.M green chilies. If you don't live in the southwest where they're sold, you can order them at The Hatch Chili Store online. They come roasted, peeled, and sealed. They're a little expensive, but they go a long way, and they make everything taste amazing! You can always roast your own on your barbeque. Just blacken the skins, cover with cold water, peel, remove the seeds, and chop. If you don't want to go to that much trouble, you can buy canned green chili in the grocery store. If you've never tasted fresh, then you'll think the cans taste great.

Servings depend on size of portions. You can always double recipes.

Many of these recipes I've gotten from friends across the country. Some from old cookbooks. I can't remember who I got most of them from, so I'm sorry if I can't credit you for them. Of course, I've put my own twist on them, as we all do. Enjoy!

Recipe Table of Contents

Main Dishes Beef

Green Chili Steak

INGREDIENTS:

1 round steak (cut into 1/4 to 1/2 inch pieces
2 medium tomatoes (chopped)
1 small onion
green chili to taste (1 to 2 small cans if you're not using fresh)
salt, pepper, and garlic powder to taste.

INSTRUCTIONS:

Cook on medium heat in covered frying pan. Turn to low heat after 10 minutes. Stir occasionally. If it gets dry add a little water. Cook until tender. Serve with rice.

Chicken Fried Steak with Country Gravy

(serves as many as the pieces you've cut)

INGREDIENTS:

1 round steak
cooking oil
salt
pepper
season salt (preferably Lawry's)

INSTRUCTIONS:

Cut round steak into 5 or 6 pieces. Use edge of saucer to pound steak (or buy it tenderized). Dip pieces in flour. Add spices to taste. Fry in covered frying pan (deep enough to make gravy) in about 1/4 inch of oil at medium heat until cooked through and crispy on outside. Turn and do the same on other side.

Country Gravy

INGREDIENTS:

Drippings from steak (including crispy pieces of coating)
Small amount of oil if not enough drippings
Whole or 2% milk (amount depends on how much drippings you have and how much gravy you want).
Salt and pepper to taste

INSTRUCTIONS:

Heat frying pan you cooked steak in. Add flour (about 1/3 cup or more depending on how much drippings you have) stirring constantly with a whisk. When flour is medium brown and bubbly add milk. Start with 2 to 3 cups stirring vigorously until starts to thicken. Add more milk if gravy is too thick. When it comes to rolling boil turn down heat and let gravy cook at a low boil for several minutes. This keeps it from having that floury taste.

Roast Beef with Mushroom Gravy

INGREDIENTS:

1 boneless chuck roast (meat will shrink considerably in cooking)
2 to 3 cans Cream of Mushroom soup (depending on size of roast)
1 pkg. Lipton dried onion soup (a little less for small roast)

about 3/4 soup can of water

INSTRUCTIONS:

Mix soups and water in bottom of roasting pan. Place roast in mixture then turn over so mixture is on both sides. Cook covered at 350 degrees for about 2 hours. Roast should be very tender. If the gravy has boiled dry add water and stir. Serve over Minute Rice or mashed potatoes. Absolutely delicious! To cook in crockpot, follow directions above, cooking on high for an hour. Turn down to medium and cook for 3 to 4 hrs. (until very tender).

Roast Beef with Vegetables

INGREDIENTS:

1 boneless chuck roast
1 pkg. Lipton dried onion soup
3 to 5 peeled and halved potatoes
3 to 5 peeled carrots in 3 inch lengths cut in the middle lengthwise
about 1 cup water (maybe more—remember it's roasting not boiling)
salt and pepper to taste

INSTRUCTIONS:

At bottom of roasting pan, stir soup into water. Place roast in pan. Turn so mixture is on both sides. Cook (covered) in oven at 350 degrees for about 30 minutes. Add potatoes and carrots. Cook another 1 and 1/2 hrs. or until very tender.

Easy Beef Stroganoff

Ingredients:

1 lb. hamburger

2 cans Campbell's Cream of Mushroom soup

1 16oz. carton sour cream

1 pkg. Reames Homestyle frozen noodles

Instructions:

Fry hamburger, drain. Add soup. Cook at medium-low heat stirring often until mixture boils for several minutes. Turn off heat and add sour cream. Serve over cooked noodles.

Green-chili Meat for Burritos or Navajo Tacos

Ingredients:

1 chuck roast

2 onions

7 to 10 pods fresh garlic

3 small tomatoes chopped (Roma or that size)

green chili to taste (2 to 3 small cans—fresh is better). Cans marked "mild" don't have much heat at all. You can mix hot and mild.

about 1/3 cup cooking oil

flour (not more than 1 c.)

salt to taste

tortillas if you're making burritos

Instructions:

Boil roast in covered pot with 1 quartered onion (if you have time you can cook in a crockpot overnight), 3 to 4 pods of fresh garlic (tip: hit pods with cup or glass, peels easier).

Cook until you can pull it apart easily with a fork. Save broth. Shred cooled meat fine. In frying pan place: oil, 1 chopped onion, 4 to 6 pods garlic (minced), tomatoes (chopped), and finely chopped green chili. Chili varies so much, you have to adjust it to your taste. If I don't need all of it, I freeze it. Cook for 5 to 10 minutes. Add part of it to shredded meat, taste, add more if you need it until it's the right temperature for you. Make gravy by heating 3 to 4 cups roast broth in frying pan. Make thickening in small bowl: about 1/2 c. flour and 1c. water. Stir with whisk until lumps are out. Pour slowly into boiling broth stirring rapidly with whisk so it won't be lumpy. If gravy isn't thick enough make more thickening. If it's too thick add more broth or water. Pour enough gravy in meat to make it moist. For burritos, fill tortillas and fold. For Navajo Tacos, spread on Navajo Fry Bread.

Navajo Fry Bread

INGREDIENTS:

- 4 c. flour
- 1 TBS. baking powder
- 1 tsp. salt
- 2 TBS. powdered milk
- 1 1/2 cup warm water

INSTRUCTIONS:

Have paper towels spread on counter for draining. Mix flour, baking powder, salt, and milk. Add water and blend. Mix with hands until soft and loses most of it's stickiness. Make small balls of dough (depending on how big you want your piece). Roll balls to about 1/16 in. thickness. Fry on both sides in 1/2 in. hot oil until light brown. Use tongs to remove. Place on paper towels. Serve with butter and honey, green-chili meat; or hamburger, lettuce, and tomatoes like a taco.

Taco Salad

INGREDIENTS:

about ½ head iceberg lettuce
2 or 3 medium tomatoes (chopped)
2 or 3 chopped green onions (green stems included)
1/2 to 1 c. cheese (grated)
1 lb. hamburger
1 can kidney beans (drained)
1 pkg. Schilling taco seasoning
taco flavored tortilla chips
salsa (optional)

INSTRUCTIONS:

Place lettuce, tomatoes, green onions, and cheese in large bowl. Brown hamburger in frying pan (drain grease carefully). Add drained kidney beans and Schilling taco seasoning. Stir and heat through. Add hamburger mixture and chips to lettuce mixture right before serving. Individuals can top with salsa if they wish.

Main Dishes Chicken

Chicken Tacos

INGREDIENTS:

1 boiled and finely shredded chicken
1/2 c. green onions (chopped)
1 c. finely sliced celery
2 medium tomatoes (chopped)
salt, pepper, cumin to taste
about 1 to 1 and 1/2 dozen crispy or soft fried taco shells
1 to 2 c. grated cheese (your choice, I prefer cheddar)
optional: shredded lettuce, additional chopped tomatoes, and salsa to top tacos

INSTRUCTIONS:

Sauté vegetables and seasonings until celery is tender. Add shredded chicken. Stir and cook about 1 minute. Fill fried taco shells. Top with cheese. Put in oven for a few minutes to melt cheese. Top with lettuce, tomatoes, and salsa if desired. Great without toppings as well.

Chicken Enchiladas

INGREDIENTS:

1 boiled, shredded chicken (save broth)
1 16 oz. carton sour cream
2 cans Campbell's Cream of Chicken Soup
Chopped green chilis to taste (2 to 3 small cans if you're not using fresh. You can mix mild and hot to your taste)
1 tsp. salt

1/2 tsp. pepper
1/4 tsp. garlic powder (not garlic salt)
12 to 16 soft-fried corn tortillas
1/2 onion cut in 2 wedges
2 c. mild or medium cheddar cheese

INSTRUCTIONS:

Boil chicken with wedges of onion and a little salt. Cool and shred.

Put all ingredients except cheese and tortillas into large pot. Slow boil on low heat and stir often to keep from scorching. If too thick to spread easily, add a little of the chicken broth. CAREFULLY soft-fry tortillas in less than an inch of hot oil, placing them on paper towels to soak up grease. In casserole dish, spread thin layer of chicken mixture. Layer tortillas (tear to fit edges), cheese, and chicken mixture. Repeat until mixture is gone, ending with cheese. Cover casserole dish with tinfoil. Place in oven at 350 degrees for 20 to 30 minutes (until thoroughly heated), removing tinfoil for last 5 minutes. Yummy!!!

Chicken Broccoli Casserole

INGREDIENTS:

2 10 oz. pkgs. frozen broccoli (better yet, cook fresh broccoli)
4 c. deboned boiled chicken
2 cans Campbell's Cream of Chicken Soup (no substitutes, please!)
3/4 c. mayonnaise
1/2 c. mild cheddar cheese

1 c. soft bread crumbs (2 or three slices of bread)
1 TBS. melted butter

INSTRUCTIONS:

Cook broccoli until tender, drain. Arrange stalks in greased baking dish. Layer chicken on top. Combine soup, mayonnaise, and cheese. Pour over chicken. Sprinkle with cheese. Combine crumbs and butter. Sprinkle over all. Bake at 350 for 35 minutes or until heated through.

Chicken and Rice San Francisco Style

INGREDIENTS:

1 boiled shredded chicken (save broth)
2 regular size chicken Rice-a-Roni (you can use 3 for more servings without using more chicken)
2 TBS. butter or margarine per box
2 1/2 c. broth per box (if there's not enough broth use water for remainder)

INSTRUCTIONS:

In a large skillet, combine rice-vermicelli mix and butter or margarine. Sauté over medium heat until vermicelli is golden brown, stirring frequently. Slowly stir in broth and special seasonings (comes in box) and shredded chicken; bring to a boil. Cover and reduce heat to low. Simmer 15 to 20 minutes until rice is tender. Do not stir! Do not open lid often. Rice should be moist but not soup-y. Cook until excess liquid has evaporated.

Fried Chicken

Ingredients:

chicken parts (bone-in tastes best)
cooking oil
2 to 3 eggs (cracked and whipped with fork)
flour (to coat chicken)
salt and pepper

Instructions:

Wash and salt chicken parts. Dip in eggs then flour. Place chicken in 1/2 to 3/4 in. medium hot oil. Salt and pepper. Cover pan. Fry about 10 minutes on one side. Turn (carefully) salt and pepper on other side. Keeping pan covered, cook for about 10 minutes. Turn heat down to medium. Turn 2 or 3 times until golden brown. Make sure chicken is thoroughly cooked. Great with mashed potatoes and country gravy.

Bread

Homemade Biscuits

INGREDIENTS:

4 c. flour (self-rising)
1/4 c. Crisco shortening (not oil)
1 and 3/4 to 2 c. milk

INSTRUCTIONS:

Cut flour into shortening using pastry cutter or a fork until mixed evenly. Add milk a little at a time. Dough will be slightly sticky. Put flour on your hands. Knead 3 or 4 times. If its too sticky sprinkle a little more flour on it. Put dough on floured surface. Roll out with rolling pin or pat with hands to about 1/2 in. thickness. Cut biscuits with a drinking glass. Preheat oven (important!). Bake on lightly greased cooking sheet at 375 to 400 degrees until light brown. Make gravy by country gravy recipe substituting bacon grease for drippings.

Hush Puppies

INGREDIENTS:

2 c. cornmeal (may be part flour)
2 tsp. baking powder
1 tsp. salt
2 TBS. finely chopped onion
cooking oil
1 beaten egg
3/4 c. milk (enough to make a thick batter)

Instructions:

Mix dry ingredients. Add and blend in onion, egg, and milk. Drop by teaspoonful into hot oil and fry to a golden brown. Drain on paper towels and serve hot.

Blueberry Muffins

Ingredients:

2 c. flour
3 tsp. baking powder
1/3 c. sugar
1 tsp. salt
1 c. milk
2 beaten eggs
1 TBS. cooking oil
1 c. blueberries

Instructions:

Blend dry ingredients. Stir in milk, eggs, and oil. Wash and drain blueberries then dust with 1 TBS. flour and stir into batter. Turn into greased muffin pans, filling no more than 2/3 full. Preheat oven to 425 degrees. Bake for 25 to 30 minutes.

Sopapillas

Ingredients:

2 c. flour
1 TBS. baking powder
1/2 tsp. salt
1 TBS. shortening
cooking oil

2/3 c. lukewarm water
optional: butter and honey

Instructions:

Blend dry ingredients until resembles cornmeal. Gradually add water, stirring with fork (dough will be crumbly). Turn onto floured surface. Knead into smooth ball. Divide dough in half. Let stand 10 minutes. Roll each half into 12 and 1/2 x10 in. rectangles. Cut into 2 and 1/2 in. squares (don't reroll or patch dough). Fry a few at a time in deep hot oil. Serve with butter and honey.

Month-old Bran Muffins

This muffin mix can be kept in the refrigerator for 4 to 5 weeks. Just spoon out what you want to cook and cover tightly. Do not stir once in container.

Ingredients:

2 c. 100 percent bran
4 c. All Bran cereal
2 c. boiling water
2 and 1/4 c. sugar
1 c. shortening
4 beaten eggs
5 c. flour
5 tsp. baking soda
1 and 1/2 tsp. salt
1 qt. buttermilk
1 lb. chopped dates

Instructions:

Mix bran and boiling water. Let stand. Cream together sugar, shortening, eggs. Stir together flour, baking soda, salt. Add flour mixture, 1 qt. buttermilk, and bran mixture to creamed mixture. Fold in All Bran and chopped dates. Bake at 375 degrees for 20 minutes. Can be baked in microwave muffin pan in microwave.

Soups

Chicken and Rice Green Chili Soup

INGREDIENTS:

1 shredded whole boiled chicken (save broth)

3 or 4 Wyler's chicken bouillon cubes (nothing but Wyler's)

Hatch's green chili to taste (can use 1 to 2 small cans of green chili. See note about Hatch's chilies at beginning of recipe book).

about 1 c. uncooked Minute Rice

a few shakes of each of the following (to taste)

salt

pepper

cumin

oregano

garlic powder

sweet basil

INSTRUCTIONS:

Boil and debone chicken (save broth).

Add water to desired amount of soup if not enough broth. Add bouillon cubes and green chili to taste. Add rice according to how much soup you're making. Add spices. Slow boil until rice is tender.

Chicken Noodle Soup

INGREDIENTS:

1 whole chicken (boiled and shredded—save broth)

3 or 4 Wyler's chicken bouillon cubes
1 pkg. Reames frozen noodles
salt and pepper

Instructions:

Cover chicken completely in salted water. Boil. Cool. Shred. If not enough broth, add some water to equal desired amount of soup. Add 3 to 4 bouillon cubes, salt, and pepper. Add shredded chicken and noodles (separate with fork as they are boiling). Cook until noodles are tender.

Beef Stew

Ingredients:

1 and 1/2 lbs. stew meat
The following vegetables in desired amounts:
potatoes
carrots
celery
onion (at least 1)
canned corn
1 lg. can tomatoes
optional: zucchini, macaroni, okra
salt and pepper

Instructions:

Boil salted meat for about an hour. Add vegetables in desired amounts. Boil for another hour or two. Cook down two or three times adding water. The longer and slower you cook it the more the flavors will mingle. Can be cooked in crockpot.

Potato Soup

Ingredients:

5 to 6 medium potatoes (peeled and cut into 1 in. squares)
about 3 strips of cooked bacon (save grease)
1 small onion diced
salt and pepper
1/2 cube butter (more if you like)
milk (2 to 3 c.)
thickening (flour and water the consistency of cream)

Instructions:

Fry bacon. Drain on paper towel, break into small pieces (save grease).

Boil cubed potatoes with bacon pieces and a little bacon grease, onion, salt, and pepper. Cook until potatoes are soft. Do not drain. Water should be at least 2 inches above potatoes. Add milk and butter. Bring to boil stirring bottom. When boiling, quickly stir small streams of thickening into mixture with a whisk until thickened to the consistency of cream. Lower heat. Cook (stirring occasionally) until water and milk have boiled down and some of the potatoes have dissolved into the liquid. Salt and pepper to taste. It takes a lot of salt.

Desserts

Peach Cobbler

Ingredients:

4 c. sliced peaches (preferably fresh, can use berries)
1 c. sugar (to taste)
1c. flour
1 tsp. baking powder
1/4 c. sugar (additional)
1/8 tsp. salt
1 beaten egg
1 c. milk
2 TBS. cooking oil

Instructions:

Place peaches in buttered baking dish. Sprinkle 1 c. sugar evenly over fruit. Blend flour, baking powder, 1/4 c. sugar, and salt. Blend beaten egg, milk, and oil. Add to dry ingredients and beat to smooth batter. Pour batter over fruit and bake at 350 degrees for 40 minutes. Serve warm. Great with vanilla ice cream.

Mississippi Mud Cake

Ingredients:

2 c. sugar
1 and 1/2 c. all-purpose flour
1 c. shortening
4 whole eggs
1/3 c. Hershey's cocoa

3 tsp. vanilla
1 c. chopped pecans or walnuts
1/4 tsp. salt
1/2 pkg. miniature marshmallows

INSTRUCTIONS:

Cream shortening and sugar. Add eggs and beat by hand. Mix flour, cocoa, and salt. Add to creamed mixture. Add vanilla and nuts. Mix well. Pour into greased and floured cake pan and bake at 35 minutes at 300 degrees. Take out of oven and pour on marshmallows. Put back in oven at 350 degrees for 10 minutes. Cool and spread icing.

Icing

INGREDIENTS:

1 or 2 sticks melted butter or margarine
1/3 c. cocoa
1 box powdered sugar
1/2 c. powdered sugar
1/2 c. evaporated milk
1 tsp. vanilla
1 cup chopped pecans or walnuts

INSTRUCTIONS:

Mix powdered sugar and cocoa, then mix well with melted butter. Add evaporated milk, vanilla and nuts. Spread on cake.

Pie Crust

Ingredients:

2 and 1/2 c. Gold Medal All Purpose flour
1 c. Crisco shortening
1 tsp. salt
cold water

Instructions:

Cut shortening into flour and salt with pastry cutter or fork until crumbly. Add water very little at a time until dough just barely holds together. Roll out half of dough with floured rolling pin on floured surface to about 1/8 in. (or less) thickness. Do not overwork dough (the secret to flakey crust is to handle it as little as possible—if you can pick it up in one piece it is not going to be flakey). Run long knife under dough to loosen. Place dough in pie pan. Press into pan, piecing together as necessary. Crimp edges. Poke bottom and sides with fork. Repeat with other half of dough. Bake at 350 degrees for 20 minutes or until golden brown.

Banana Cream Pie Filling

Ingredients:

1 lg. pkg. Jell-O Cook and Serve Vanilla Pudding mix for each pie crust. If you're making 2 pies, you can use 2 lg. and 1 sm. packages of pudding to make sure you have a full crust.
2 medium bananas for each pie crust
3 c. 2% or whole milk per pie crust
1 pint whipping cream for each pie
sugar

1 tsp. vanilla

INSTRUCTIONS:

Cook according to directions on pkg. Be sure to cook in a thick-bottomed pan because pudding can scorch easily. When pudding is barely warm stir in sliced bananas. Spread into pie crust. Whip cream with electric mixer until almost stiff. Stop. Add sugar to taste and 1 tsp. vanilla to cream. Whip only long enough to mix. Spread on cooled pie and serve.

You can make chocolate pie using Jell-O Chocolate Cook and Serve Pudding.

Blueberry Dessert

INGREDIENTS FOR CRUST:

2 c. flour
2 cubes margarine or butter
1/3 c. brown sugar
1/2 c. chopped pecans
Ingredients for filling:
1 lg. pkg. cream cheese
1 c. powdered sugar
1/2 c. powdered sugar
1 lg. pkg. Dream Whip
cold milk (amount according to Dream Whip pkg.)
1 can blueberry pie filling

INSTRUCTIONS:

Combine ingredients for crust. Bake 20 to 25 minutes at 350 degrees. Crumble to use. Save enough to garnish top of dessert. For filling, combine cream cheese and powdered sugar. Whip 1 lg. pkg. dream whip. When stiff add 1/2 c. powdered sugar. Mix Dream Whip and cream cheese mixture. Smooth over crumbled crust. Spread pie filling over all. Top with crumbled crust. Chill.

Jell-O Cake

INGREDIENTS:

1 white cake mix
1 pkg. Dream Whip
1 lg. pkg. Jell-O Instant Vanilla Pudding
1 sm. pkg. strawberry Jell-O
enough milk to bring pudding and Dream Whip to the consistency of frosting

INSTRUCTIONS:

Bake cake according to instructions on pkg. Mix Dream Whip and instant pudding (powder), using enough milk to bring to the consistency of frosting. Using a fork, poke holes in entire cake about 1 in. apart. Prepare Jell-O according to pkg. but do not chill. Pour over cake. Top with pudding mixture.

Chocolate Pudding Cake

INGREDIENTS:

1 chocolate cake mix
1 lg. pkg. Jell-O Cook and Serve Chocolate Pudding
1 pkg. Cool Whip

Instructions:

Mix cake according to directions. Spread in cake pan. Cook pudding. While still hot, smooth over uncooked cake mix. Bake according to directions on pkg. Cool. Top with Cool Whip.

Cowboy Cookies

Ingredients:

2 c. shortening
2 c. brown sugar
2 c. white sugar
4 eggs
4 c. white flour
2 tsp. baking soda
2 tsp. salt
1 tsp. baking powder
4 TBS. milk
4 c. old-fashioned oats
4 tsp. vanilla
1 pkg. chocolate chips

Instructions:

Add flour, baking soda, baking powder, and salt to mixture. Stir well. Add beaten eggs, then oats, vanilla, and milk. Stir well. Add chocolate chips. Stir. Drop by large spoonsful on baking sheet. Bake at 350 degrees until light brown. Do not overcook.

Best-in-the-world Brownies

INGREDIENTS:

1 and 1/2 c. flour
1 c. cooking oil (no olive)
4 to 5 TBS. Hershey's cocoa
2 c. sugar
4 eggs
1/2 to 1 c. chopped pecans
1 tsp. baking powder
1 tsp. salt
2 tsp. vanilla

INSTRUCTIONS:

Mix and bake at 325 degrees for 30 to 40 minutes. Top with icing while still warm. Great served with vanilla ice cream. These brownies are extremely moist. Must eat with a fork.

Dump Cake

INGREDIENTS:

1 20 oz. can crushed pineapple with juice
1 21 oz. can cherry pie filling
1 pkg. yellow cake mix
1 c. chopped pecan or walnuts
1-2 sticks of butter cut into slices

INSTRUCTIONS:

Preheat oven to 350 degrees. Grease 13x9" cake pan. Dump pineapple with juice into pan, spreading evenly. Dump pie filling into pan, spreading evenly. Sprinkle box of dry cake mix evenly over cherry layer. Top with pecan or walnut pieces. Bake 45 to 50 minutes or until top is golden brown. Best served hot with vanilla ice cream.

Apple Crisp

INGREDIENTS:

1 c. flour
1.c. sugar
1 egg
2 TBS. cinnamon/sugar
1/3 c. oil
about 12 apples (a little tart)

INSTRUCTIONS:

Cover bottom of pan with peeled, sliced apples. Sprinkle with 1 TBS. cinnamon/sugar. Mix flour, egg, and sugar to crumbly stage. Cover all the apples. Pour oil evenly over topping and sprinkle with remaining cinnamon/sugar. Bake at 350 degrees for 30 minutes. Best served warm with vanilla ice cream.

Candy

Lemon Drops

Ingredients:

1 c. powdered sugar
lemon juice

Instructions:

Pour enough lemon juice into the powdered sugar to dissolve it. Cook to hard-crack stage, or 275 degrees F. on candy thermometer. Drop onto buttered cookie sheet to cool and harden.

Caramel Popcorn Balls

Ingredients:

Popcorn (about 1 to 2 gallons)
1 tsp. salt
1 cube margarine or butter
1 c. light Karo syrup
2 and 2/3 c. brown sugar
1 can Eagle Brand milk (regular)
1 tsp. vanilla

Instructions:

Have large platter ready for finished popcorn balls. Pop the corn. Better if air-popped. Combine all ingredients and cook to soft-ball stage (after the caramel comes to a boil, you start dropping a small spoonful into a small bowl filled with very cold water in intervals a few minutes apart. At first, the caramel is shapeless, but after several tests, it starts to hold its shape. When it reaches the stage that it can be formed into a soft ball and lifted from water, then you know it's ready. If you cook it too little it won't hold the popcorn together. Too much and it will be crackly). Pour over popcorn and stir until all is covered. Turn on cold-water faucet and leave running. Put your hands under the water then grab enough caramel popcorn to form a ball. Press it into a ball quickly. Put hands under water again. Repeat until all popcorn is gone. Be careful. The caramel is very hot and will burn your hands if you don't have cold water on them.

The Original Fantasy Fudge

INGREDIENTS:

3 c. white sugar
3/4 c. butter or margarine
2/3 c. evaporated milk
1 (12 oz.) pkg. semisweet chocolate chips
1 (7 oz. jar Kraft marshmallow crème
1 c. chopped walnuts
1 tsp. vanilla

INSTRUCTIONS:

Mix sugar, butter, and evaporated milk in large, heavy saucepan. Cook over medium heat, stirring to dissolve sugar. Bring mixture to a full boil for 5 minutes, stirring constantly. Remove from heat and stir in chocolate chips until melted and thoroughly combined. Beat in marshmallow crème, walnuts, and vanilla. Pour into buttered cake pan. Let cool before cutting into squares.

How to Help the Author

Thank you for reading *I was a Stranger: A Guide to Biblical Hospitality*. I hope you enjoyed it. If you would like to help, I'd appreciate it if you'd leave a review on Amazon. More than any other thing, reviews help authors spread the word about their books. And they help readers find the books they love. It doesn't have to be long or eloquent. Just a few sentences about how the book made you feel. Please create your review here.

Get Marilyn's book

The Struggle for Love: The Story of Leah

on Amazon

Two sisters married
to the same man.
A man who loves only one.

Leah didn't want a marriage without love. A strong and capable woman, she had determined to live a life of service as a midwife, bringing other women's children into the world, allowing her father to breach tradition and betroth her beautiful younger sister first. But that was not to be.

Forced by her father to pose as her sister, Leah goes to Jacob's wedding bed. When Jacob awakens to find Leah instead of the beautiful Rachel, he tells Leah that he will provide for her and do what a husband must, but she will never have his love.

Rejected by her husband and her relationship with her beloved sister broken, will Leah be able to keep her faith in the God of Abraham through the tragedies to come? Will Jacob see Leah for the woman she truly is? Will these two wives of the patriarch mend their relationship before it's too late?

Enjoy this beautiful story of a woman overlooked by history but not by God. In Genesis 29:31 the scripture says, "When the Lord saw that Leah was not loved—" God was watching over Leah. And He's watching over you.

ABOUT THE AUTHOR

Marilyn has worn many hats: pastor's wife, mother of four God-loving children, school teacher, author and blogger—to name a few. Four years after becoming a widow, she married Peter Parker. Yes, she's Mrs. Spiderman! How cool is that! When she and her husband are not out RVing, they reside in Buckeye, Arizona, with their dog Mimi. She (Marilyn, not Mimi!) is presently the older, more wrinkled half of a mother/daughter blogging duo with her daughter, Rebecca. Their website, Persevering Women, is full of stories that inspire women to realize how much they are loved and cared for by their Creator. Marilyn's greatest desire is that her work reflect the glory and goodness of God.

Printed in Great Britain
by Amazon

18700946R00062